I0110512

THE ULTIMATE
KID'S TRAVEL
JOURNAL AND TRIP PLANNER!

Activinotes

Activinotes

DAILY JOURNALS, PLANNERS, NOTEBOOKS AND OTHER BLANK BOOKS

Copyright 2016

All Rights reserved. No part of this book may be reproduced or used in any way or form or by any means whether electronic or mechanical, this means that you cannot record or photocopy any material ideas or tips that are provided in this book.

This Book Belongs To

_____

My Fun Trip Journal

To....

_____

Date:

___ / ___ / ___

My Trip Journal

Where we started this Morning...

Where were stopping tonight...

Something I ate today...

Something I saw today...

Something I learned today...

My favorite thing about this day...

Today I Visited...

Today I went to...

First,

Next,

Then,

Finally

I had a great time because...

Vacation Planning

I am going to...

I am travelling by...

I am staying in...

I am going with...

Sticky Pics of My Trip...

Sticky Pics of My Trip...

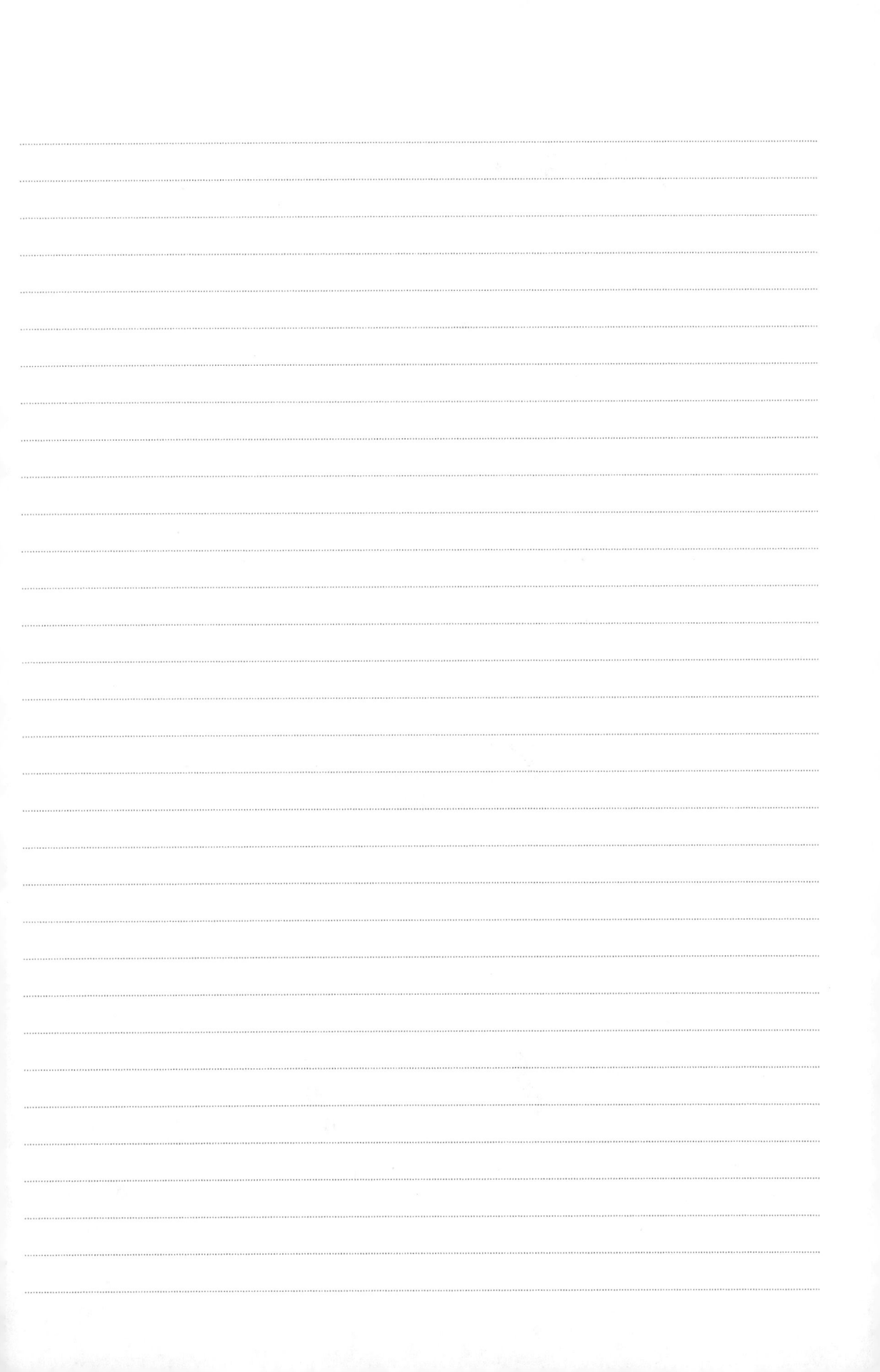

My Fun Trip Journal

To....

_____

Date:

____/____/____

My Trip Journal

Where we started this Morning...

Where were stopping tonight...

Something I ate today...

Something I saw today...

Something I learned today...

My favorite thing about this day...

Today I Visited...

Today I went to...

First,

Next,

Then,

Finally

I had a great time because...

Vacation Planning

I am going to...

I am travelling by...

I am staying in...

I am going with...

Sticky Pics of My Trip...

Sticky Pics of My Trip...

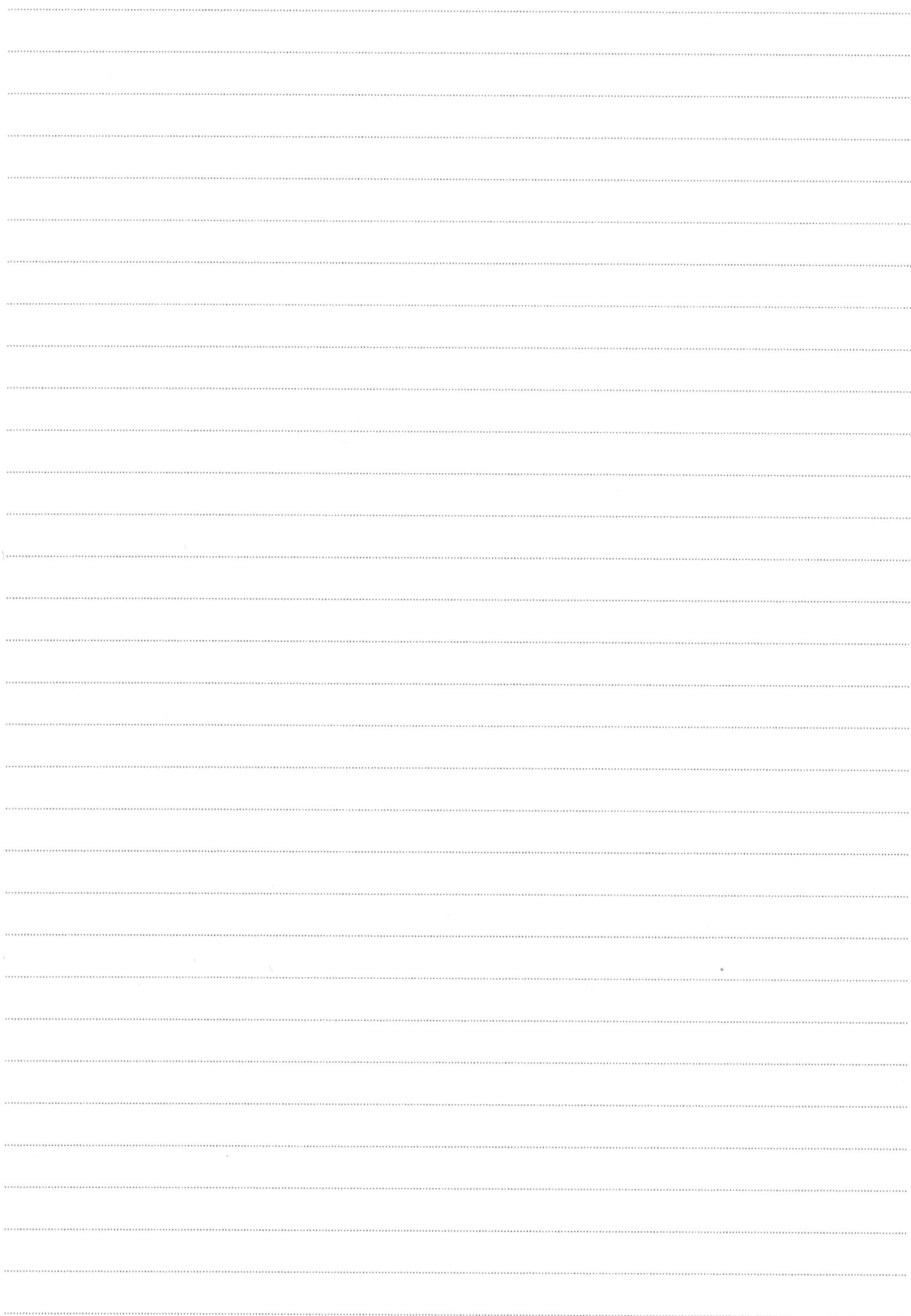

My Fun Trip Journal

To....

_____

Date:

____/____/____

My Trip Journal

Where we started this Morning...

Where were stopping tonight...

Something I ate today...

Something I saw today...

Something I learned today...

My favorite thing about this day...

Today I Visited...

Today I went to...

First,

Next,

Then,

Finally

I had a great time because...

Vacation Planning

I am going to...

I am travelling by...

I am staying in...

I am going with...

Sticky Pics of My Trip...

Sticky Pics of My Trip...

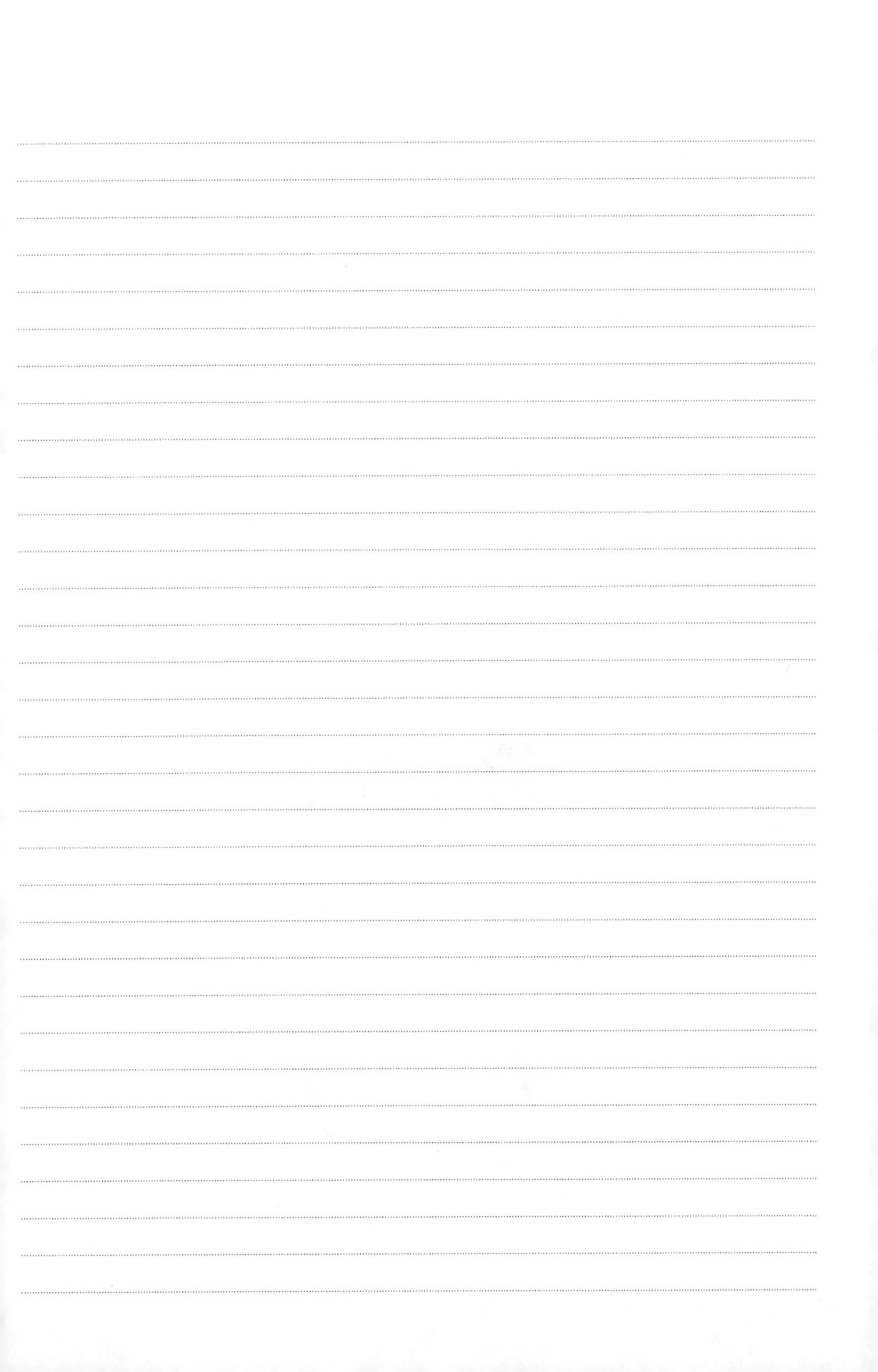

My Fun Trip Journal

To....

_____

Date:

___/___/___

My Trip Journal

Where we started this Morning...

Where were stopping tonight...

Something I ate today...

Something I saw today...

Something I learned today...

My favorite thing about this day...

Today I Visited...

Today I went to...

First,

Next,

Then,

Finally

I had a great time because...

Vacation Planning

I am going to...

I am travelling by...

I am staying in...

I am going with...

Sticky Pics of My Trip...

Sticky Pics of My Trip...

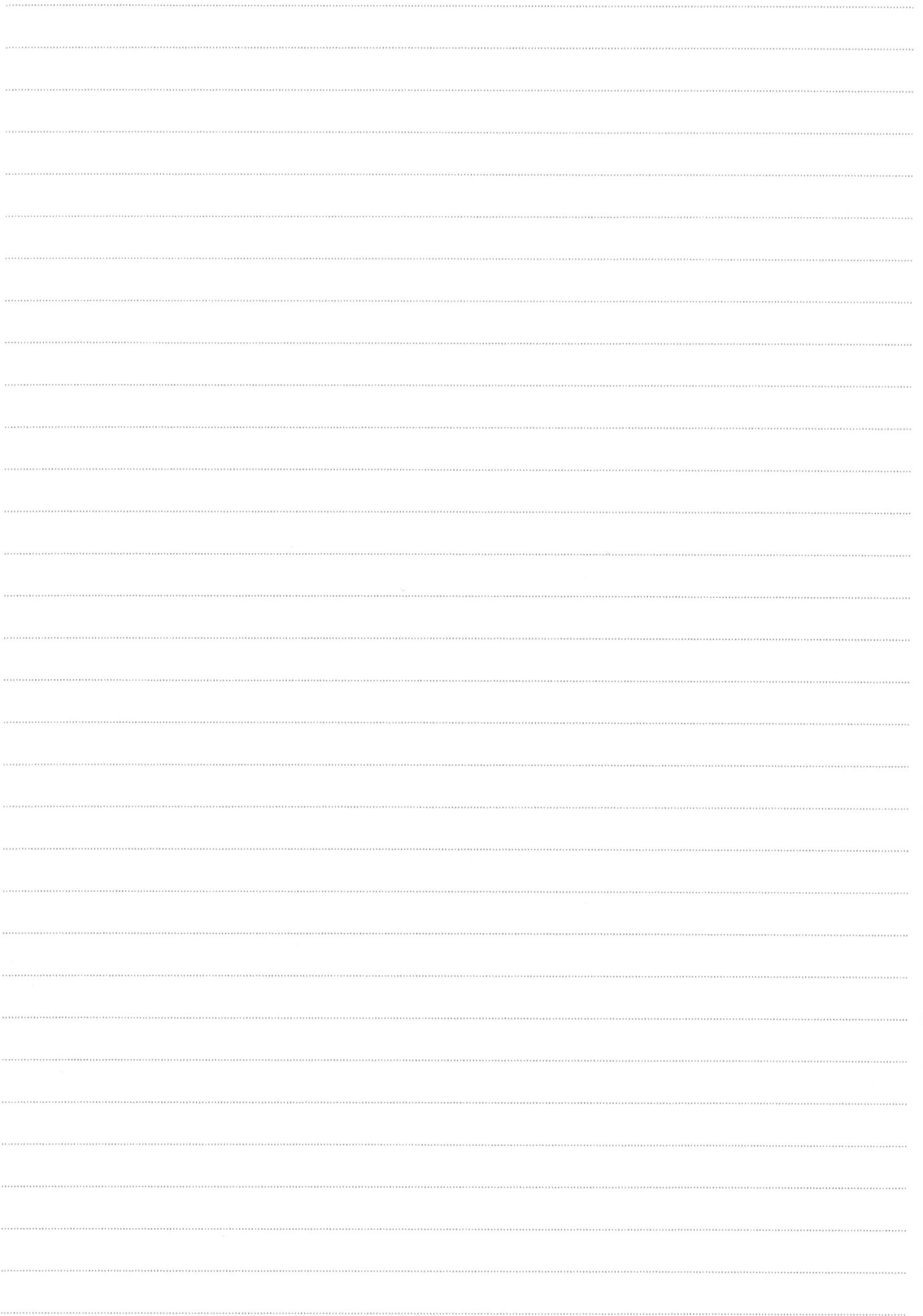

My Fun Trip Journal

To....

_____

Date:

___/___/___

My Trip Journal

Where we started this Morning...

Where were stopping tonight...

Something I ate today...

Something I saw today...

Something I learned today...

My favorite thing about this day...

Today I Visited...

Today I went to...

First,

Next,

Then,

Finally

I had a great time because...

Vacation Planning

I am going to...

I am travelling by...

I am staying in...

I am going with...

Sticky Pics of My Trip...

Sticky Pics of My Trip...

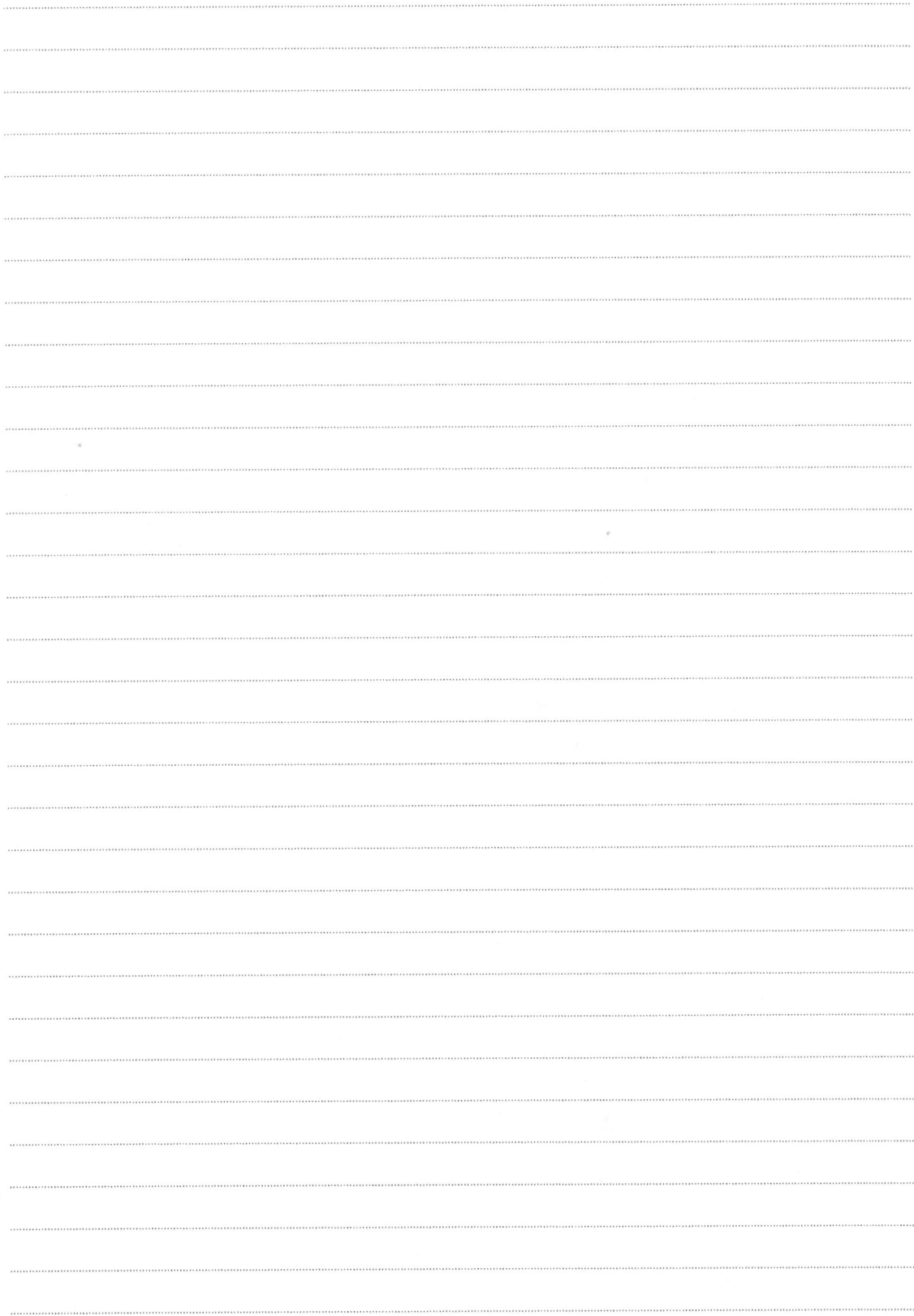

My Fun Trip Journal

To....

_____

Date:

_____/_____/_____

My Trip Journal

Where we started this Morning...

Where were stopping tonight...

Something I ate today...

Something I saw today...

Something I learned today...

My favorite thing about this day...

Today I Visited...

Today I went to...

First,

Next,

Then,

Finally

I had a great time because...

Vacation Planning

I am going to...

I am travelling by...

I am staying in...

I am going with...

Sticky Pics of My Trip...

Sticky Pics of My Trip...

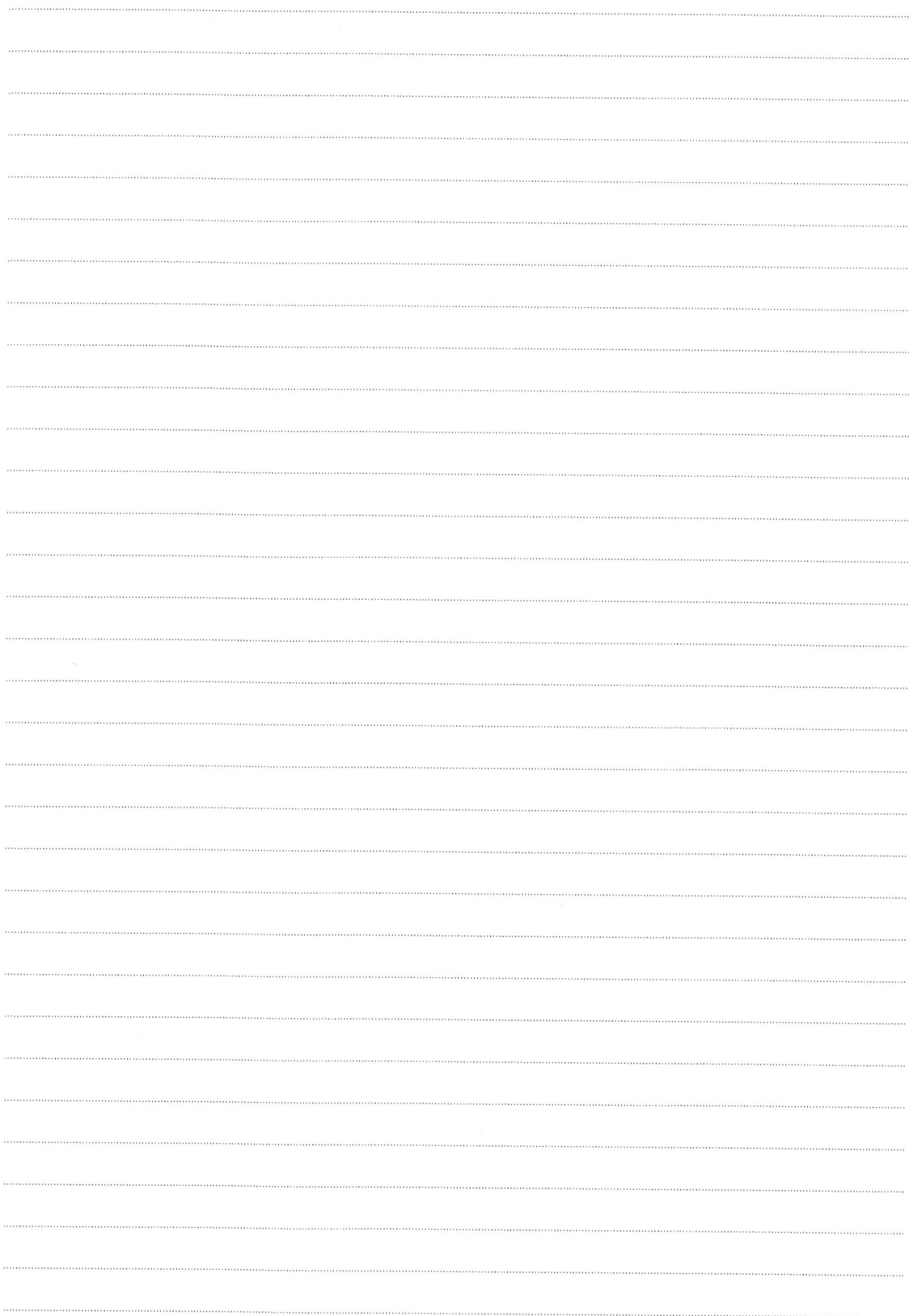

My Fun Trip Journal

To....

_____

Date:

____/____/____

My Trip Journal

Where we started this Morning...

Where were stopping tonight...

Something I ate today...

Something I saw today...

Something I learned today...

My favorite thing about this day...

Today I Visited...

Today I went to...

First,

Next,

Then,

Finally

I had a great time because...

Vacation Planning

I am going to...

I am travelling by...

I am staying in...

I am going with...

Sticky Pics of My Trip...

Sticky Pics of My Trip...

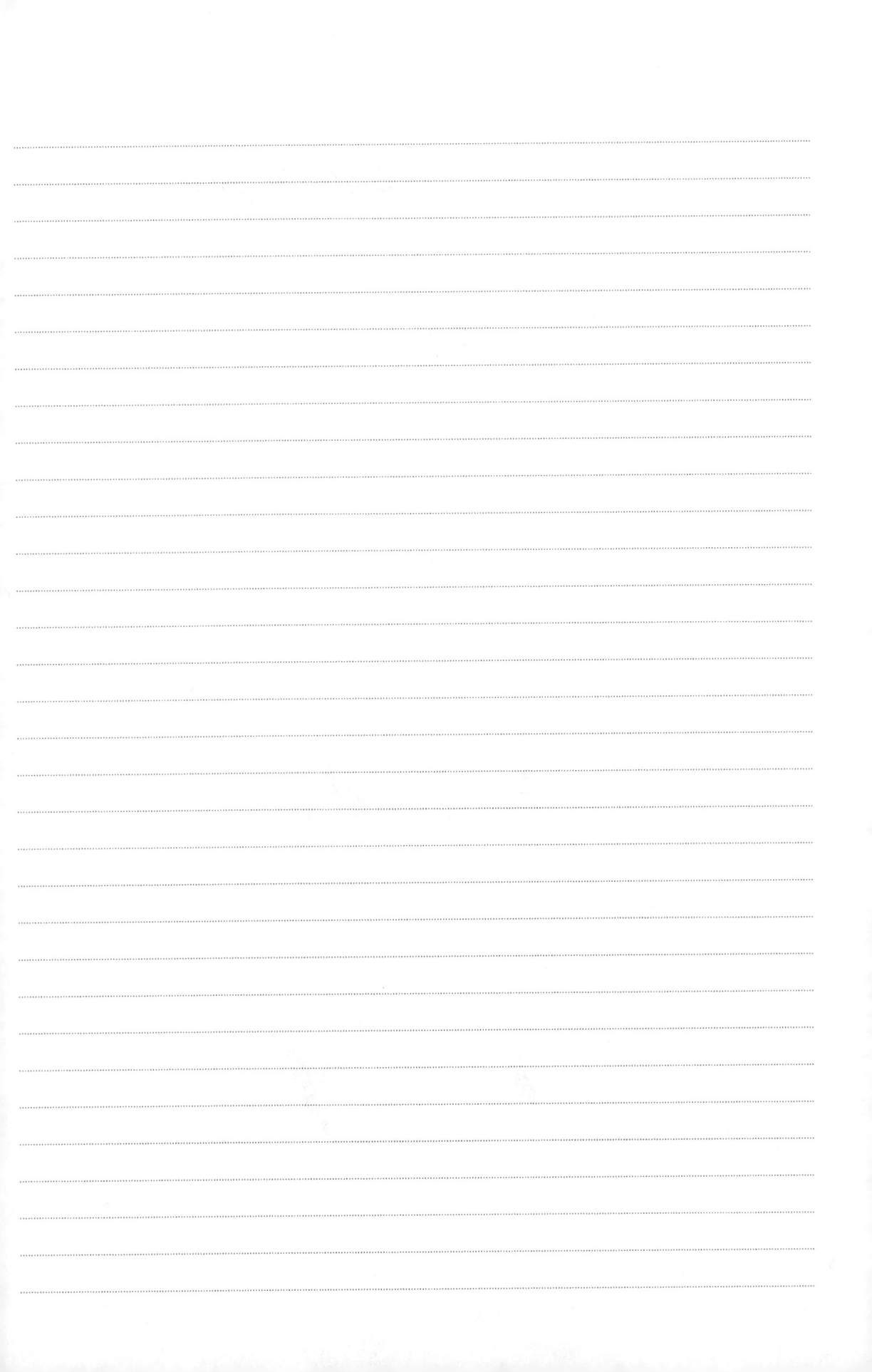

My Fun Trip Journal

To....

_____

Date:

____/____/____

My Trip Journal

Where we started this Morning...

Where were stopping tonight...

Something I ate today...

Something I saw today...

Something I learned today...

My favorite thing about this day...

Today I Visited...

Today I went to...

First,

Next,

Then,

Finally

I had a great time because...

Vacation Planning

I am going to...

I am travelling by...

I am staying in...

I am going with...

Sticky Pics of My Trip...

Sticky Pics of My Trip...

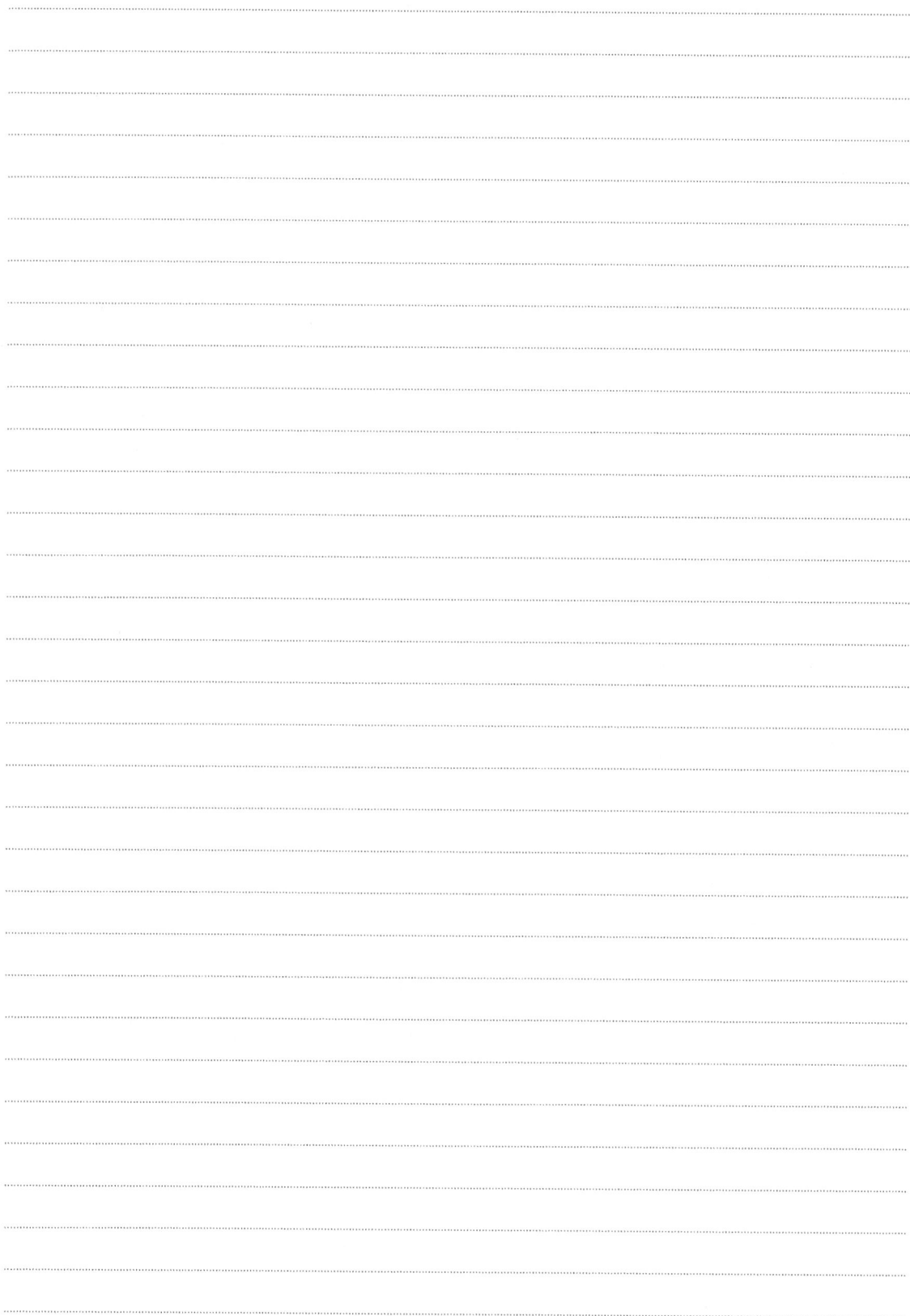

My Fun Trip Journal

To....

_____

Date:

___/___/___

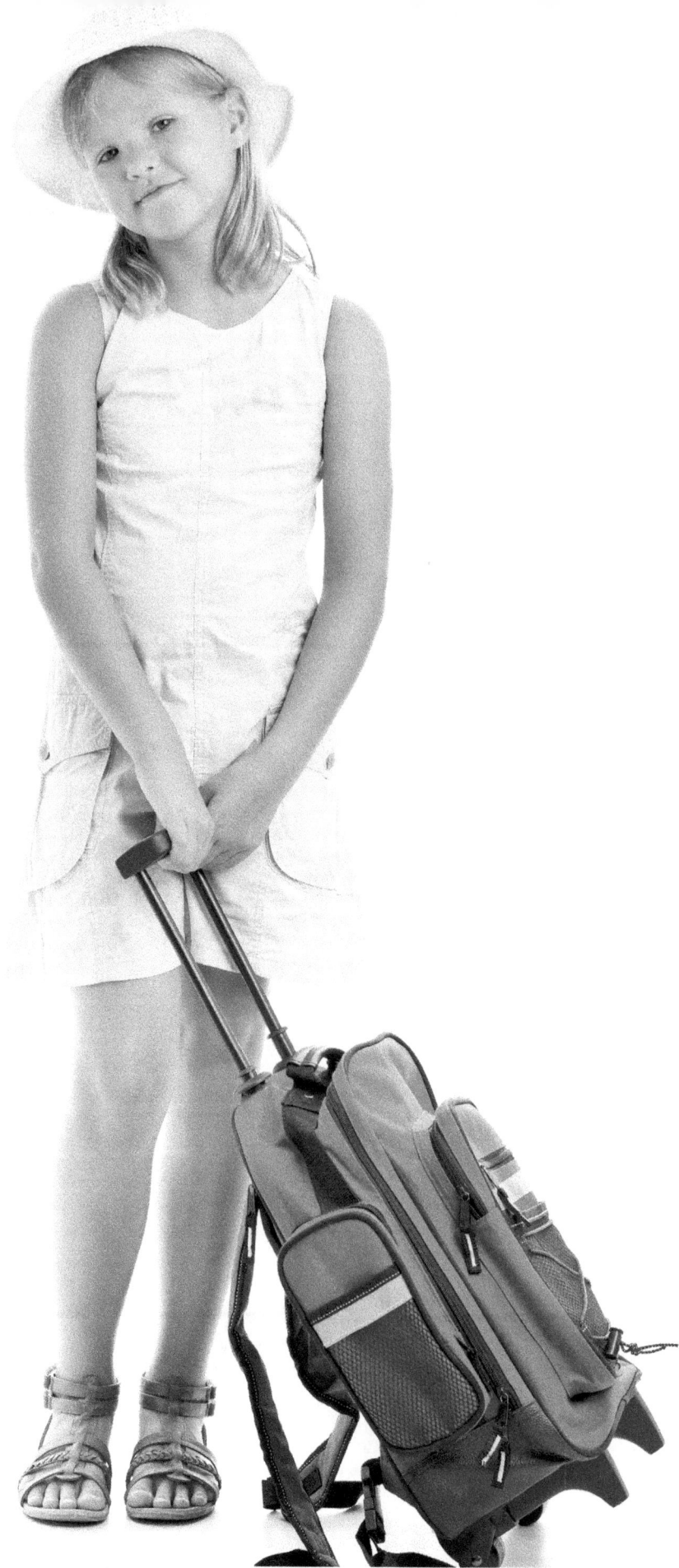

My Trip Journal

Where we started this Morning...

Where were stopping tonight...

Something I ate today...

Something I saw today...

Something I learned today...

My favorite thing about this day...

Today I Visited...

Today I went to...

First,

Next,

Then,

Finally

I had a great time because...

Vacation Planning

I am going to...

I am travelling by...

I am staying in...

I am going with...

Sticky Pics of My Trip...

Sticky Pics of My Trip...

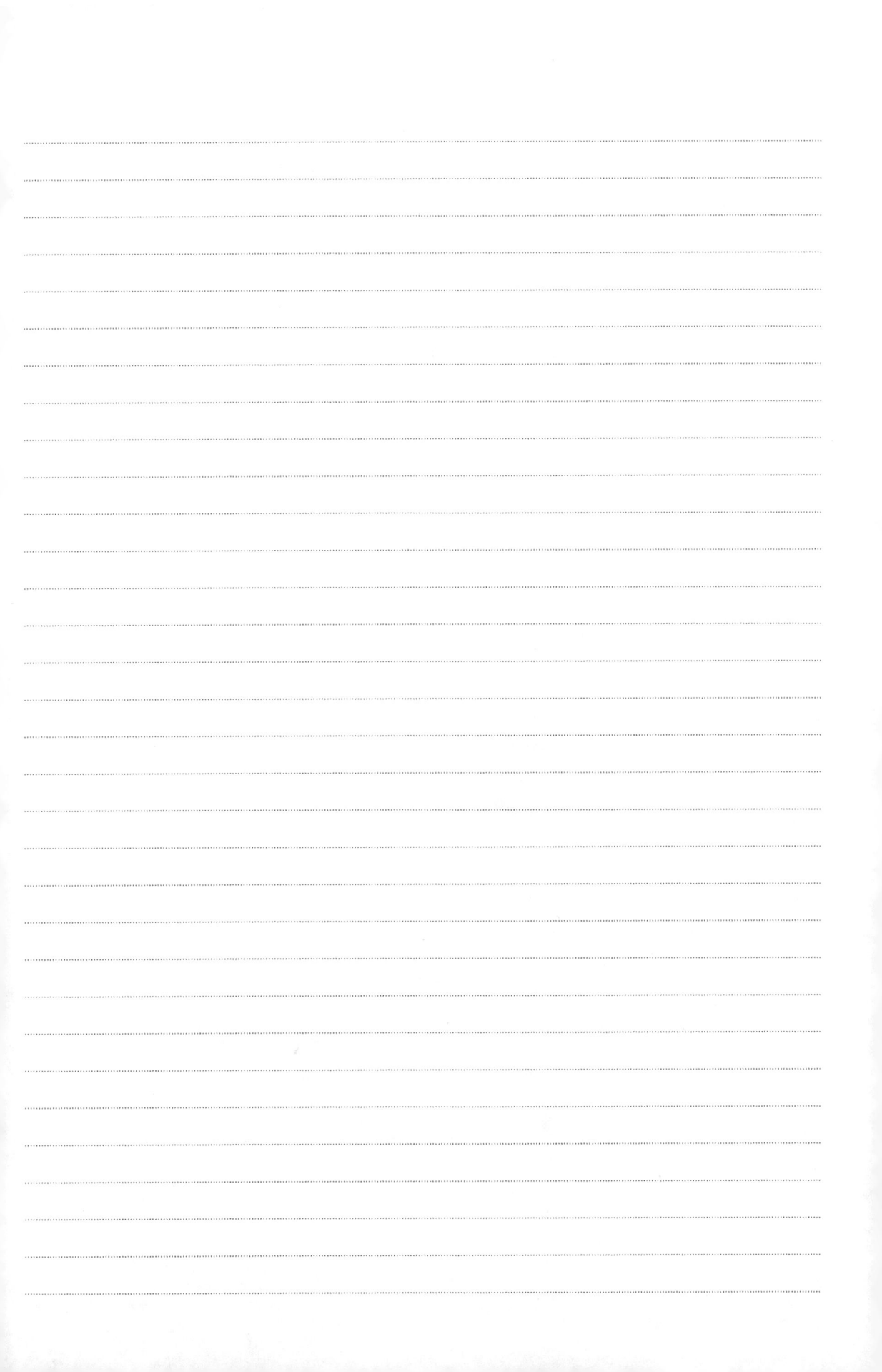

My Fun Trip Journal

To....

_____

Date:

_____/_____/_____

My Trip Journal

Where we started this Morning...

Where were stopping tonight...

Something I ate today...

Something I saw today...

Something I learned today...

My favorite thing about this day...

Today I Visited...

Today I went to...

First,

Next,

Then,

Finally

I had a great time because...

Vacation Planning

I am going to...

I am travelling by...

I am staying in...

I am going with...

Sticky Pics of My Trip...

Sticky Pics of My Trip...

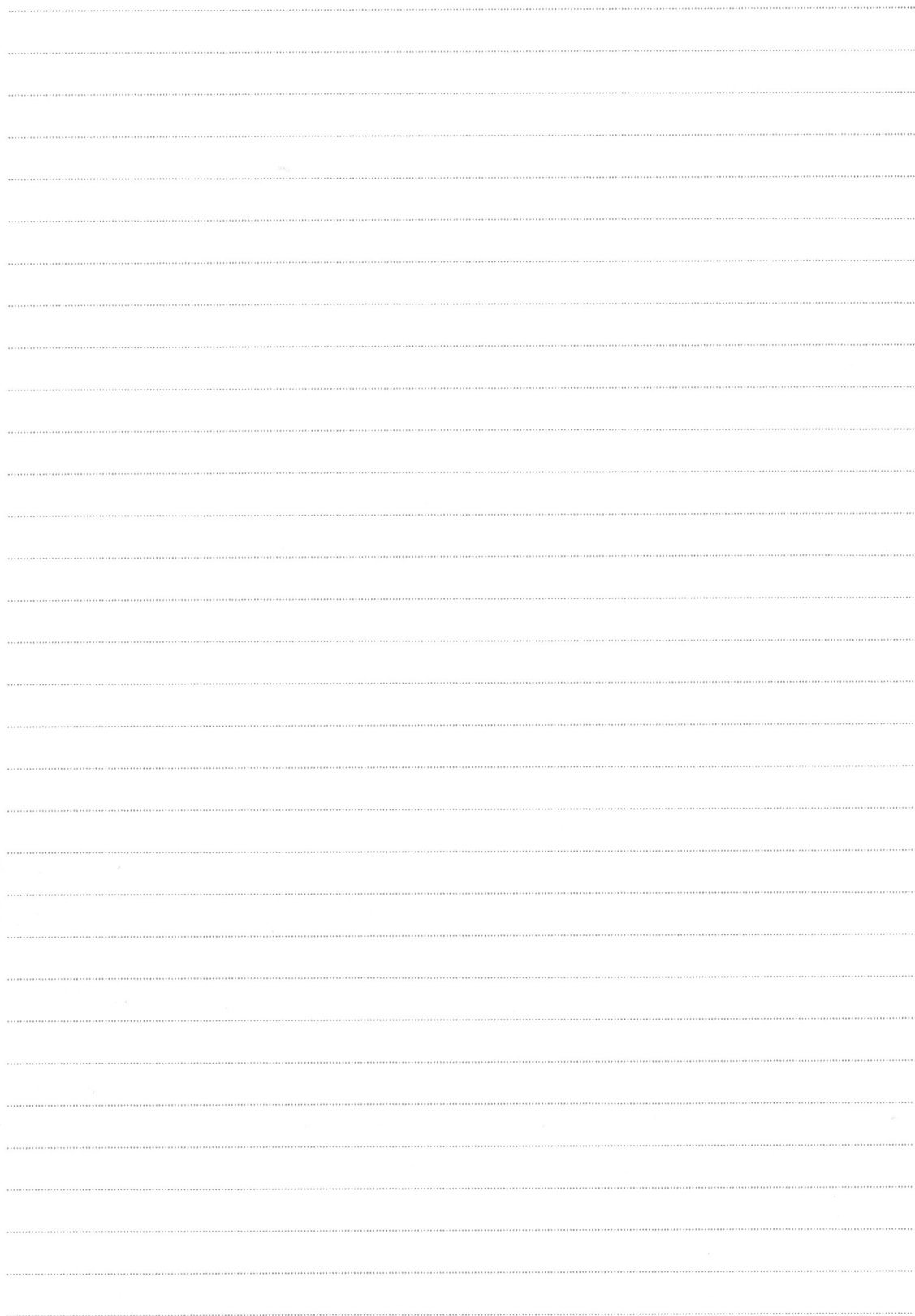

www.ingramcontent.com/pod-product-compliance
Lightning Source LLC
Chambersburg PA
CBHW081338090426

42737CB00017B/3192